Connie Matricardi is a craft designer, former elementary school art teacher and longtime puppet enthusiast. She has designed several lines of hand and finger puppets and has performed for young audiences in elementary classrooms, preschools and daycare centers.

"Bringing a puppet ~~to life away to the child~~ holds such magic. I'm always amazed how read ~~~~ ~~~~ uppet play and how much they share in that mag ~~~~

D1365575

Acknowled~~gements~~

"I thank nursery school teacher Sue Lever, kindergarten ~~~~ Suzi Manger and Peggy West and daycare mother Jackie Yeagley for sharing their valuable experiences concerning finger plays and preschoolers. I also thank their children, ages 18 months to six years, for their spontaneous and honest reactions."

Children and Puppet Plays

"Who's that tripping over my bridge?"

"What, lost your mittens? You naughty kittens!"

"They sailed away for a year and a day..."

"Two little blackbirds sitting on a hill..."

▶ These are probably some of the best-loved lines in western culture, fondly remembered because they were shared over and over again in a spirit of fun.

Puppet plays are a delightful way to pass on favorite stories, poems and songs to the next generation. These soft, bright-colored, easy-to-make puppets make great story tellers and can give structure and appeal to quiet time, whether in the classroom or on a long car ride. Puppet story time can be especially rich for the young child enjoying for the first time the playfulness of rhythm and rhyme.

Puppet plays invite participation. Try performing "Five Little Monkeys Jumping on the Bed." By the second verse the children will be reciting along with you! Kindergarten teachers have found these puppets a wonderful way to focus a group after play time. In addition to counting, monkey puppets and the three little kittens can be used to introduce primary colors. Any of the puppets can also be used on a flannel board.

From old favorites to new rhymes about fussy babies and moon creatures, we hope you enjoy this collection of puppet plays and share them often!

PUBLISHED BY
PAT DEPKE BOOKS
Quality Craft Instructions
New Windsor, MD 21776-0779

PUBLISHER
Herb Depke

EDITOR
Victoria Crenson

ART COORDINATOR
PUBLICATION DESIGNER
Jan Gilbert Hurst

PHOTOGRAPHER
T.R. Wailes

Two little blackbirds sitting on a hill,
One named Jack, the other named Jill.
Fly away, Jack! Fly away, Jill!
Come back, Jack! Come back, Jill!

Two little blackbirds sitting on a gate,
One comes early, the other comes late.
Fly away, Early! Fly away, Late!
Come back, Early! Come back, Late!

Two little blackbirds sitting on a cloud
One named Soft, the other named LOUD!
Fly away Soft! Fly away, Loud!
Come back, Soft! Come back, Loud!

Two little blackbirds, sitting in the snow.
One named Fast, the other named Slow.
Fly away, Fast! Fly away, Slow!
Come back, Fast! Come back, Slow!

Daycare providers have found this finger play helps ease some of the anxiety children feel being separated from their parents. The birds disappear but then always return.

Older children recognize the concept of opposites and love to whisper along with Soft and shout with Loud.

 See page 21 for puppet instructions.

Three Little Kittens

Three little kittens
  they lost their mittens,
And they began to cry,
"Oh! Mother dear,
We very much fear,
Our mittens we have lost."

"What? Lost your mittens, you naughty kittens!
Then you shall have no pie.
  Mee-ow, mee-ow, mee-ow.
Yes, you shall have no pie.
  Mee-ow, mee-ow, mee-ow."

The three little kittens found their mittens,
And they began to cry,
"Oh! Mother dear,
See here, see here!
Our mittens we have found!"

"What? Found your mittens, you p e r r r fect kittens!
Then you shall have some pie.
  Purr, purr, purr.
Yes, you shall have some pie.
  Purr, purr, purr."

Kittens are two-sided—one side with mittens, one side without. Kindergartners may enjoy a puppet variation: glue on Velcro dots so the mittens are removable. Children can then practice matching color pairs.

To make their own pair of mittens to color, trace little hands on paper with fingers together.

▶ See page 27 for puppet instructions.

The Owl and the Pussycat went to sea
    In a beautiful pea-green boat,
They took some honey, and plenty of money,
    Wrapped up in a five-pound note.
The Owl looked up to the stars above,
    And sang to a small guitar,
"O lovely Pussy! O Pussy, my love,
    What a beautiful Pussy you are
        You are,
        You are!
    What a beautiful Pussy you are!"

Pussy said to the Owl, "You elegant fowl!
    How charmingly sweet you sing!
O let us be married! too long we have tarried:
    But what shall we do for a ring?"
They sailed away, for a year and a day,
    To the land where the Bong-tree grows,
And there in a wood a Piggy-wig stood
    With a ring at the end of his nose,
        His nose,
        His nose,
    With a ring at the end of his nose.

"Dear Pig, are you willing to sell for one shilling
    Your ring?" Said the Piggy, "I will."
So they took it away, and were married next day
    By the Turkey who lives on the hill.
They dined on mince, and slices of quince,
    Which they ate with a runcible spoon;
And hand in hand, on the edge of the sand,
    They danced by the light of the moon,
        The moon,
        The moon,
    They danced by the light of the moon.

by Edward Lear

Children love the sound of the words and the dreamlike images of this night-time enchantment. We may not understand the meaning of "runcible spoon," but Lear's non-sense poem has the comforting lilt of a lullaby.

See page 28 for puppet instructions.

The Lion and the Mouse

One day a Lion was sleeping in the tall grass when a tiny Mouse ran over his back. The Lion was annoyed to be awakened from his nap. He opened one eye, grabbed the tiny Mouse in his big paws and was about to eat her.

"Oh please, mighty Lion," squeaked the frightened Mouse, "do not eat me. If you let me go I will repay your kindness one day."

The Lion laughed at the idea of a puny mouse helping a big, powerful lion. "I'll let you go, funny mouse." The Mouse scurried away into the tall grass.

Later the Lion was caught in a net laid by some hunters. The Lion roared in anger and rolled about in the tall grass. The more he struggled, the more tangled in the ropes he became.

The tiny Mouse heard the Lion's roars. She hurried to see what was the matter. When she saw the Lion's predicament, she began to gnaw at the ropes of the net. One-by-one the ropes fell away until the Lion was free.

No matter what size you are, you can be a help, even to the biggest and strongest.

by Aesop

See page 26 for puppet instructions.

Throughout the centuries this simple fable has retained its tremendous popularity for all ages. Its appeal for young children is clear in the message: even the littlest in the family can be a big help. "How do you help at your house?"

Staging tips: When the lion captures the mouse, he can hold the puppet's yarn tail between his paws. A piece of brown twine wrapped around the lion makes a convincing net trap. Make a second mouse puppet and stage another popular fable from Aesop—"Town Mouse and the Country Mouse."

Moon Creatures Party

Way, way up in the night time sky,
Moon creatures dance and eat moon pie,
Bounce up and down to a loud moon beat
Whistle moon songs through holes in their feet.

Stomp! Stomp! Stomp!   *(stamp feet)*
Chomp! Chomp! Chomp!   *(clap hands)*
Whistle moon songs through holes in their feet!   *(say along)*

Moon creatures like their pie ice cold   *(hug self and shiver)*
Shivery blue and three days old,   *(hold up three fingers)*
With a pinch of pink pudding and a cup of green punch.
Nothing tastes better than a yummy moon munch.   *(rub tummy)*

Munch! Munch! Munch!   *(say along)*
Crunch! Crunch! Crunch!
Nothing tastes better than a yummy moon munch.   *(rub tummy)*

Moon creatures giggle when they bounce up high
Eyes wiggle round to see the sky   *(draw circles in the air)*
Jump moon mountains in one big leap.   *(reach up high)*
When the sun comes up, they go to sleep.   *(rest cheek on hands)*

Yawn! Yawn! Yawn!   *(say along)*
Zzzz! Zzzz! Zzzz!
When the sun comes up, they go to sleep.   *(rest cheek on hands)*

by Victoria Crenson
Copyright © 1993 Victoria Crenson

Children have fun stamping and clapping along with this catchy lunar rhythm.
Perhaps your kids can invent a moon creature dance or their own recipes for "moon pie."

▶ See page 32 for puppet instructions.

Ben Bear

All morning the rain pattered against the windows.
Ben Bear watched the puddles in the yard get fatter
and fatter.

"I want to jump in those puddles," he told his
mother. "I'm going outside to play."

And his Mama said...
    "Put your hat on, my darling.
      Put your hat on, my pet.
      Put your hat on, my honey bear,
      Or you will get wet."
So Ben put on his hat.
"Now I'm going outside to play," he said.

And his Mama said...
    "Put your coat on, my darling.
      Put your coat on, my pet.
      Put your coat on, my honey bear,
      Or you will get wet."
So Ben put on his coat.
"Now I'm going outside to play," he said.

And his Mama said...
    "Put your boots on, my darling.
      Put your boots on, my pet.
      Put your boots on, my honey bear,
      Or you will get wet."
So Ben put on his boots.
NOW I'm going outside to play," he said.

And his Mama said...
    "Have fun!"
So Ben went outside and splashed in all
the puddles.

And he didn't get wet!

by Victoria Crenson
Copyright © 1993 Victoria Crenson

Put your hat on, my darling. Put your hat on my pet. Put your

hat on, my honey bear or you will get wet!

See page 30 for puppet instructions.

Ben Bear hand puppet has
Velcro pieces for easy sticking
and removal of his rain suit.
    Make a scarf, winter hat, sun
hat and sunglasses and you'll
have a bear for all seasons!

Once upon a time there were three billy goats named Gruff. They were hungry goats because they'd eaten all the grass on their side of the valley and now there wasn't enough left for a good meal.

"I have an idea," said the smallest Billy Goat Gruff. "Let's go up into the hills where the grass grows thick and sweet."

"That suits me fine," said the middle-sized Billy Goat Gruff.

"Go on ahead and I'll catch up with you soon," said the biggest Billy Goat Gruff.

The smallest billy goat set off for the grassy hills. But to reach them, he had to cross a bridge over the river. Under the bridge lived a very ugly, very wicked troll.

"Trip-trip, trip-trip!" went the tiny hooves of the smallest Billy Goat Gruff as he started over the bridge.

"Who's that tripping over MY bridge," roared the wicked troll as he stuck his ugly nose over the side of the bridge.

"Oh, it is only I," answered the smallest Billy Goat Gruff.

"Well, you can be my supper," shrieked the troll. "I'm coming to eat you up!"

"I'm too little to make much of a supper for you," said the smallest Billy Goat Gruff. "Wait a bit and my big brother will be coming by."

Practice your troll voice! Children like to demand along with you, "Who's that tripping over my bridge?"

The middle-sized billy goat can be a big sister if you explain that she's really a nanny goat.

The greedy troll growled, "Very well. I'll wait. Now, get going!" and he slipped back under the bridge.

It wasn't long before *"Trip-trap, trip-trap!"* the middle-sized Billy Goat Gruff started across the bridge.

"Who's that tripping over MY bridge," yelled the troll as he stuck his ugly nose over the side of the bridge.

"It is only I," answered the middle-sized Billy Goat Gruff.

"Well, you shall be my supper!" shrieked the troll. "I'm coming to eat you up!"

"I'm not big enough to make much of a supper," said the middle-sized Billy Goat Gruff. "Wait a bit and my big brother will be coming by."

"Very well," said the wicked troll. "I'll wait a little longer. Now, get going!" and he slipped back under the bridge.

It was only a few minutes before *"Trip-trop, trip-trop!"* The biggest Billy Goat Gruff started over the bridge.

"Who's that tripping over MY bridge!" hollered the troll as he stuck his ugly nose over the side of the bridge.

"It is I!" shouted the biggest Billy Goat Gruff. "I'll cross any bridge I please."

"Well, I'm coming to eat you up," growled the wicked troll.

"Come on up, then," said the biggest Billy Goat Gruff. "You'll be sorry!"

The troll scrambled up on the bridge and tried to grab big Billy Goat Gruff. Big Billy Goat Gruff lowered his horns and charged. "Crash!" He knocked the wicked troll right off the bridge and into the river far below. He was never seen again.

Big Billy Goat Gruff trip-tropped up to the hills to join his brothers where they nibbled the grass that grew thick and sweet until all three grew big and fat.

▶ See page 24 for puppet instructions.

5

FIVE little monkeys jumping on the bed,
One fell off and bumped his head.
Mama called the doctor and the doctor said,
"No more monkeys jumping on the bed!"

4

FOUR little monkeys jumping on the bed,
One fell off and bumped her head.
Mama called the doctor and the doctor said,
"No more monkeys jumping on the bed!"

3

THREE little monkeys jumping on the bed,
One fell off and bumped his head.
Mama called the doctor and the doctor said,
"No more monkeys jumping on the bed!"

2

TWO little monkeys jumping on the bed,
One fell off and bumped her head.
Mama called the doctor and the doctor said,
"No more monkeys jumping on the bed!"

1

ONE little monkey jumping on the bed,
He fell off and bumped his head.
Mama called the doctor and the doctor said,

0

"NO MORE MONKEYS JUMPING ON THE BED!"

▶ See page 21 for puppet instructions.

This is Fussy Baby with the brand
new tooth.
    Wah! Wah! Wah!

This is Brother who sings a goofy song
    La! La! La!
to cheer up Fussy Baby with the brand
new tooth.
    Wah! Wah! Wah!

This is Sister who does a snappy tap dance
    Tap! Tap! Tap!
while Brother sings a goofy song
    La! La! La!
to cheer up Fussy Baby with the brand
new tooth.
    Wah! Wah! Wah!

This is Daddy who makes funny pig noises
    Snort! Snort! Snort!
while Sister does a snappy tap dance
    Tap! Tap! Tap!
while Brother sings a goofy song
    La! La! La!
to cheer up Fussy Baby with the brand
new tooth.
    Wah! Wah! Wah!

This is Grandma who shakes a bunny rattle
    Rattle! Rattle! Rattle!
while Daddy makes funny pig noises
    Snort! Snort! Snort!
while Sister does a snappy tap dance
    Tap! Tap! Tap!
while Brother sings a goofy song
    La! La! La!

to cheer up Fussy Baby with the brand
new tooth.
     Wah! Wah! Wah!

This is Mama who loudly hums a lullaby
     Hum! Hum! Hum!
while Grandma shakes a bunny rattle
     Rattle! Rattle! Rattle!
while Daddy makes funny pig noises
     Snort! Snort! Snort!
while Sister does a snappy tap dance
     Tap! Tap! Tap!
while Brother sings a goofy song
     La! La! La!
to cheer up Fussy Baby with the brand
new tooth.
     Wah! Wah! Wah!

This is Spot who licks the baby's toes
     Slurp! Slurp! Slurp!
while Mama hums a lullaby
     Hum! Hum! Hum!
while Grandma shakes a bunny rattle
     Rattle! Rattle! Rattle!
while Daddy makes funny pig noises
     Snort! Snort! Snort!
while Sister does a snappy tap dance
     Tap! Tap! Tap!
while Brother sings a goofy song
     La! La! La!
to cheer up Fussy Baby with the brand
new tooth.

Ha! Ha! Ha!   That tickles.

by Victoria Crenson

▶ See page 22 for puppet instructions.

Tips for Making Puppets

Puppet Patterns

To copy full-size patterns, trace the pattern pieces you need onto tracing paper. Cut out the tracing paper patterns, pin them to felt and cut out pieces.

An even easier method is to copy the pattern pages you need on a copy machine. Cut out the paper patterns, pin them to the felt and cut out pieces.

Save your patterns in an envelope for the next puppet-making session.

Cutting

When two shapes are needed—horns, eyebrows, ears, etc.—fold the felt piece in half and cut two shapes at once. Try cutting very small shapes freehand. It is easier than trying to pin very small pieces of paper pattern to the felt. Even if the shapes are not "perfect," they will be identical and may add a new dimension or personality to your puppet.

Assembly

Body: Before attaching finger puppet body shapes together, ❶ first position arms, wings, etc. between front and back pieces. ❷ Glue items to the body back, then glue or sew edges of body shapes together, leaving the bottom edge open. Be sure to leave enough room for your finger. ❸ Position head front so that it overlaps the body front about 1/2" and glue in place.

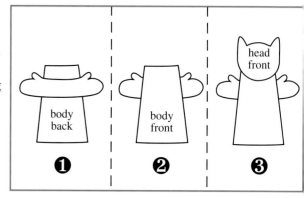

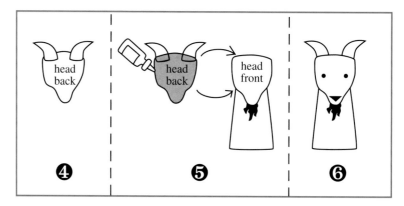

Head: ❹ Before gluing head shapes together, position hair, ears, horns, etc. between head front and back. Glue items to head back. ❺ Apply glue over entire head back and adhere it to body back as well as the front head piece. ❻ Add face details.

Gluing

A thin-bodied, white glue is recommended for gluing most felt pieces together. For best results, spread glue evenly and thinly over the entire surface to be glued out to the edges. Where a stronger bond is required, such as attaching body front to body back, use a thick tacky glue or hot glue.

Puppet bodies can also be sewn together by hand or by machine. To attach items other than felt, such as feathers, wiggle eyes, or pompoms, use tacky glue or hot glue.

Dimensional Paint

A marking pencil or disappearing ink can be used to mark lines, dots or dashes that are to be covered in dimensional paint. Allow time for paint to dry. A fine-line black marker can also be used to draw in facial features.

Reproducible Pages

See pages 33-36 for reproducible puppets to color and cut out. Wrap paper tabs loosely around child's fingers and secure with tape.

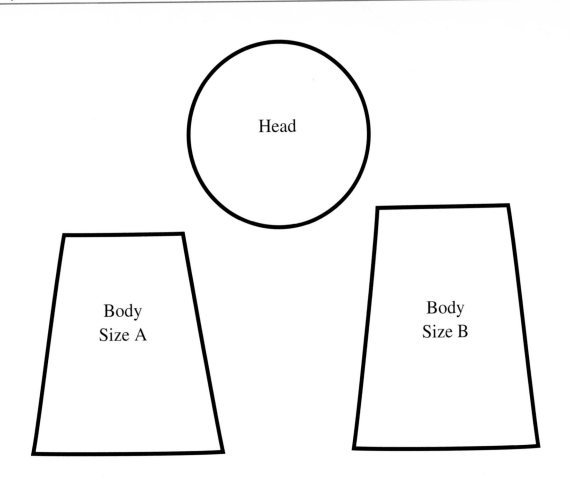

Patterns for basic finger-puppet head and bodies

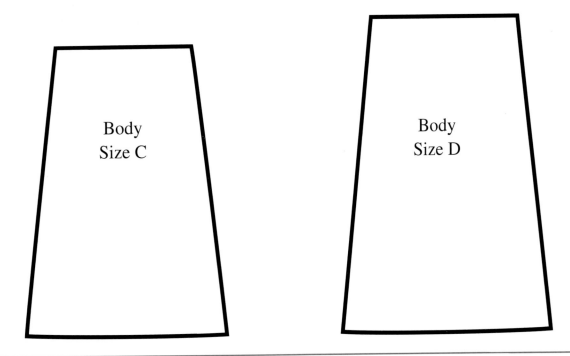

Placement for Bear Ears

Pattern for basic hand-puppet

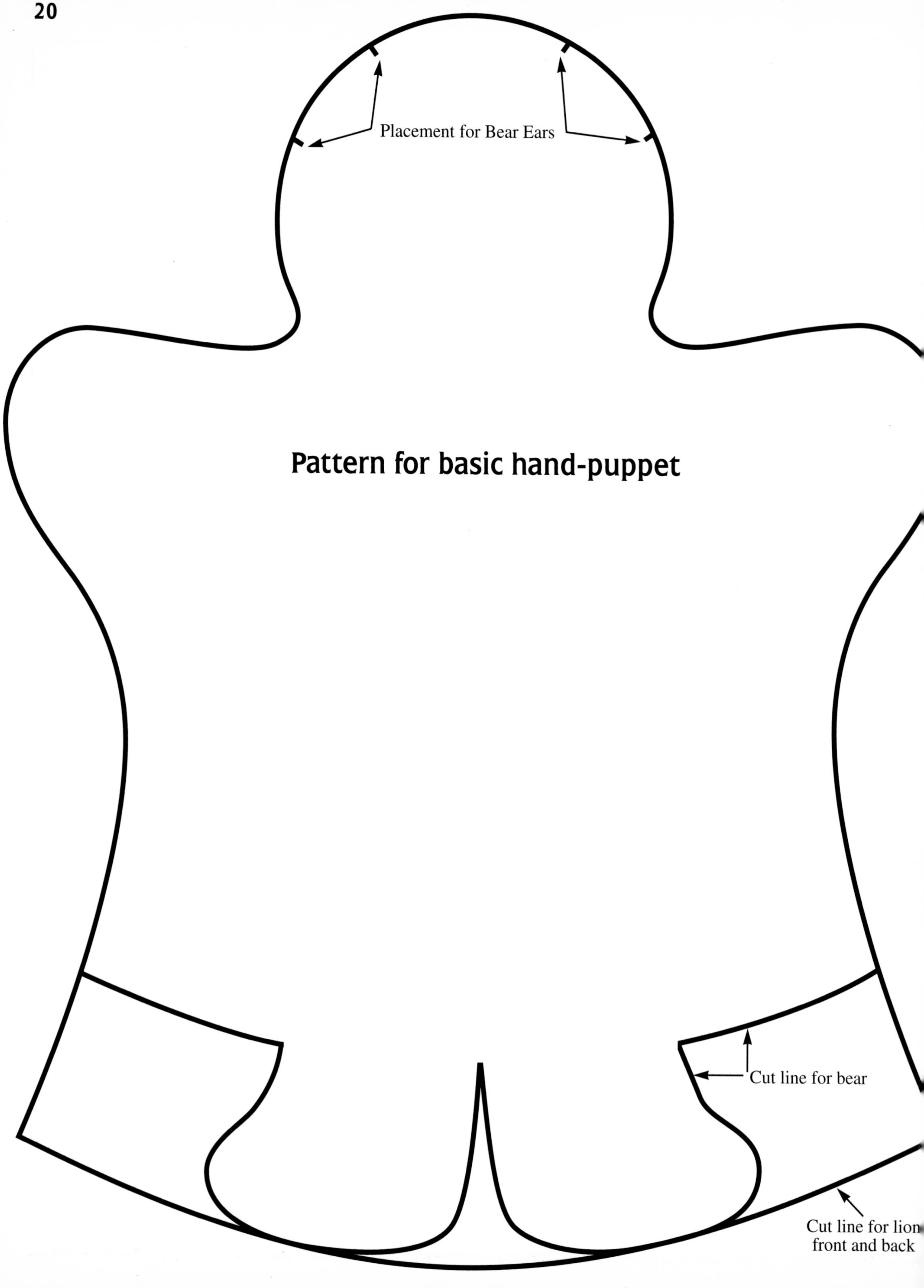

Cut line for bear

Cut line for lion
front and back

Two Little Blackbirds and Five Little Monkeys

Two Little Blackbirds

Materials:

- felt
  9"x12"—black
  4"x4"—yellow and red
- pair of wiggle eyes, 10mm
- tacky or hot glue
- black thread (optional)

Instructions:

1. To make two blackbirds, cut four size C body shapes and four head shapes (see page 19 for pattern) from **black** felt. Cut two beaks and one wing from **yellow** felt and one wing from **red** felt.

2. For each blackbird, glue or sew edges of body front to body back, leaving bottom edge open. Position beak (see photo for placement) and glue to a head shape. Glue other head shape to body front, overlapping 1/2". Glue head shapes together with beak sandwiched between them. Glue on wiggle eye and wing.

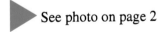 **See photo on page 2**

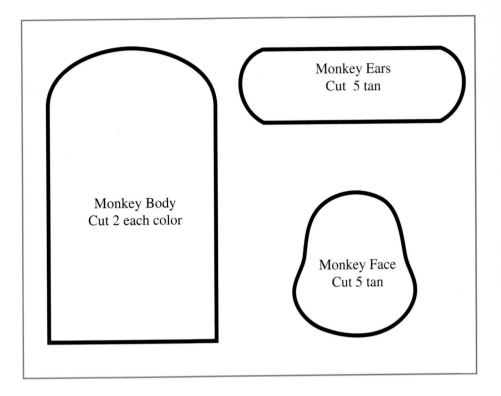

Monkey Ears
Cut 5 tan

Monkey Body
Cut 2 each color

Monkey Face
Cut 5 tan

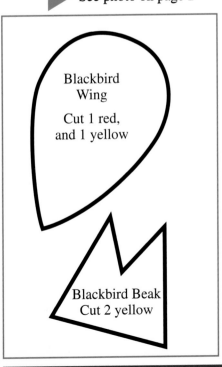

Blackbird
Wing

Cut 1 red,
and 1 yellow

Blackbird Beak
Cut 2 yellow

Five Little Monkeys

Materials:

- felt
  6"x6"—five different colors
  6"x9"—tan
- five chenille stems to match five felt colors
- dimensional paint, black
- tacky or hot glue
- thread (optional), five colors to match felt

Instructions:

1. From **each color** felt, cut two monkey body shapes. From **tan**, cut five face shapes and five ear shapes.

2. Glue ear pieces to body backs. Sew or glue edges of body fronts and backs together leaving the bottom edges open. Glue face shapes to body fronts.

3. Using dimensional paint, draw eyes, noses and mouths on faces. Glue a 3 1/2" chenille stem tail to the back of each puppet.

 **See photo on page 15**

Fussy Baby and Family

Materials:

- felt
  9"x12"sheets—white and peach
  6"x9"—black, blue, brown, gray,
     light blue, light green,
     purple, red, tan, and yellow
- 5" curly crepe wool hair, brown
- dimensional paint, black, white
- 2 pompoms, yellow, 5mm
- 4" length white ribbon, 3/8" wide
- 2 1/2" of red print ribbon, 1" wide
- two gold jump rings, 8mm
- 12" of ribbon, 1/8" wide, both
  black and white
- four wiggle eyes, 7mm
- four strands of brown yarn, 3/4"
  long
- six strands of orange-red yarn, 9"
  long
- tacky or hot glue
- black thread; white, light blue, yellow, peach and red thread (optional)

Instructions:

1. Felt Cutting Guide:
From **white** cut: two size D body
shapes, two size A body shapes, two
head shapes (see page 19 for patterns) and two diapers; from **peach**
cut: two size B body shapes, two
baby arms, four head shapes and two
sister legs; from **black** cut: one
brother hair, two sister shoes, two
dog ears, dog tail and dog nose; from
blue cut: two size D body shapes;
from **brown** cut: one head shape,
Daddy hair; from **gray** cut: one head
shape, Grandma hair; from **light blue**
cut: one head shape; from **light
green** cut: two head shapes; from
purple cut: two size D body shapes;
from **red** cut: two size C body shapes
and dog tongue; from **tan** cut: one
head shape and dog spot; from
yellow cut: two size C body shapes.

2. Baby: position and glue arms to

peach body back. Sew or glue edges
of body front and back together,
leaving bottom edge open. Glue
brown yarn strands to head back.

Glue head front to body
front overlapping felt
1/2". Glue head back to
body back. Glue one
diaper to body front and one to body
back. Glue two wiggle eyes to front
of head and two to back. Use black
dimensional paint to draw sad mouth
on one side and a happy mouth on
the other side. Be sure to let paint dry
before turning puppet over. Use
white dimensional paint to draw a
tooth on each side.

3. Brother: sew or glue
edges of red body front
and back together, leaving
the bottom edge open.
Glue head front to body
front overlapping felt 1/2". Glue hair
(also head back) to body back. Use
black dimensional paint to draw eyes
and mouth. Use white dimensional
paint to draw stripes on body front.
Let dry.

4. Sister: follow basic puppet
assembly instructions on page 18
using yellow body shapes and peach
head shapes. To make her hair, tie a
knot in the middle of orange-red yarn
strands. Glue knot to center top of
head front. Braid yarn on each side
and use narrow white ribbon to tie a
bow at each braid end. Glue yarn hair
to head. Glue black shoes to legs. Tie
small bows with black ribbon and
glue to shoes. Glue sister's legs on
inside front edge of body front. Use
black dimensional paint to draw eyes
and mouth and let dry.

5. Daddy: follow basic puppet
assembly instructions using white
body shapes and tan head shape
(front) and brown head shape (back).
Glue hair to head and red ribbon

necktie to body front. Use black
dimensional paint to draw eyes and
mouth. Let dry.

6. Grandma:
follow basic puppet
assembly instruc-
tions using purple
body shapes, light
blue head shape (front)
and gray grandma hair
shape (back.) Glue hair to
head front. Glue a yellow
pompom to either side of
face as earrings. Tie a knot in the
middle of 4" length of white ribbon.
Trim ends. Glue to right side of body
near face. Use black dimensional
paint to draw eyes and mouth. Use
white dimensional paint to draw eye-
glasses and let dry.

7. Mama: follow basic puppet
assembly instructions using blue
body shapes and light green head
shapes. Cut 5" of crepe wool and
fluff it, especially at ends. Tie a
length of black thread at mid-point of
wool. Glue center point of hair to
center top edge of head. Spread hair
to cover back of head and glue in
place. Glue a jump ring to either side
of face. Use black dimensional paint
to draw eyes and mouth. Use white
dimensional paint to make dots on
body front for necklace. Let dry.

8. Spot: follow basic puppet
assembly instructions using small
white body shapes and white head
shapes. Glue ears, nose and tongue to
head front. Glue tan circle to body
front and tail to body back. Use black
dimensional paint to draw eyes and
let dry.

▶ See "family portrait" on page 16

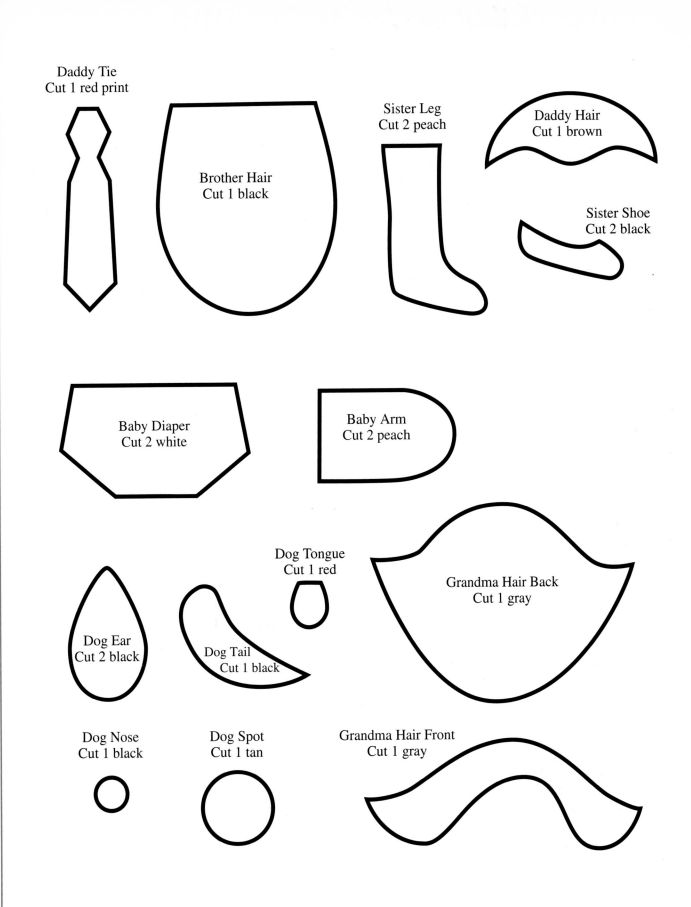

Daddy Tie
Cut 1 red print

Brother Hair
Cut 1 black

Sister Leg
Cut 2 peach

Daddy Hair
Cut 1 brown

Sister Shoe
Cut 2 black

Baby Diaper
Cut 2 white

Baby Arm
Cut 2 peach

Dog Tongue
Cut 1 red

Grandma Hair Back
Cut 1 gray

Dog Ear
Cut 2 black

Dog Tail
Cut 1 black

Dog Nose
Cut 1 black

Dog Spot
Cut 1 tan

Grandma Hair Front
Cut 1 gray

Three Billy Goats Gruff (and Troll)

Materials:

- felt
    9"x12" sheets—gray, white
    6"x9"—light blue, neon green
    very small scrap of black
- dimensional paint, black
- small pieces of fake fur, gray, white and yellow
- pair of wiggle eyes, 12mm
- glue
- thread (optional) white, gray and green
- iron-on interfacing

Instructions:

1. **Felt Cutting Guide:**
From **white** felt cut two size D body shapes, two size A body shapes (see page 19 for patterns), two small goat head shapes, two large head shapes and two medium-sized horns.
From **gray** felt cut two size B body shapes, two medium-sized head shapes, two large horns and two small horns. From **green** felt cut two troll body shapes. From **light blue** felt cut one troll head, two troll ears and a troll nose. From **black** felt cut three goat noses.

2. Glue or sew edges of body fronts and backs together, leaving bottom edges open. Position and glue horns to head shapes. Iron-on interfacing on the back of horns will make them stiffer.

Glue small piece of gray fur to back of lower head front for big goat and little goat and small piece of white fur for middle-sized goat. Glue head fronts to body fronts, overlapping felt 1/2". Glue head back to body back. Glue on noses. Draw eyes with dimensional paint and let dry.

3. To assemble troll, glue or sew edges of green body front and back together, leaving bottom edge open. Glue ears and small piece of yellow fur to back of troll's head. Glue troll head to body. Glue on nose and wiggle eyes. Use dimensional paint to draw eyebrows and mouth. Let dry.

 See photo on page 13

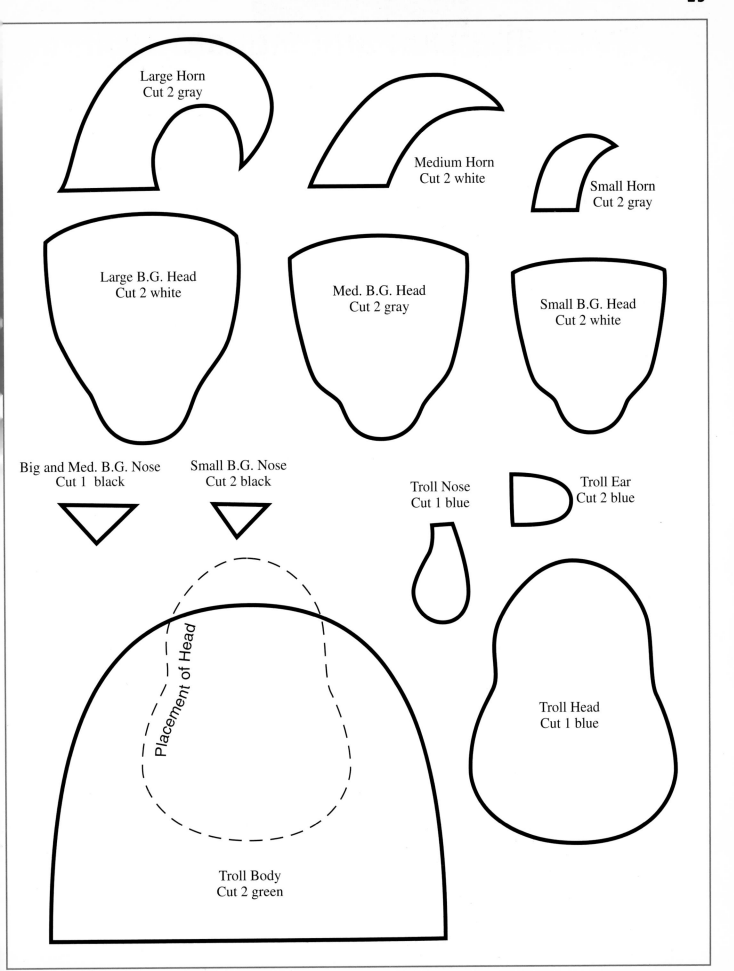

Pattern and Instructions for

The Lion and Mouse

Materials:

- felt
  two 9"x12" sheets—tan
  6"x9"—gray and tan
  4"x4"—dark brown and white
  small scrap of red
- dimensional paint, black
- 9"x12" of fake fur, dark brown
- 2 pink pompoms, 5mm
- 7" of embroidery thread, black
- two wiggle eyes, 7mm
- 6" of gray yarn
- glue
- thread (optional), gray and tan

Instructions:

1. Felt Cutting Guide:
From **tan** felt cut two lion bodies, (see page 20 for pattern) and one lion head. From **gray** felt cut two size B bodies (see page 19), two mouse heads and two mouse ears. From **dark brown** felt cut lion's eyebrows (1/4" strip), paws and nose. From **white** felt cut muzzle. From **red** felt cut small tear shape for lion's tongue. From **brown fur** cut two manes.

2. To assemble lion, glue or sew edges of body front to body back, leaving bottom edge open. Glue fur to front and back of head. Glue face over fur at front of head.

Glue white muzzle to face and tongue to muzzle. Glue on eyebrows and nose. Glue brown paw circles to hands. Use dimensional paint to draw eyes and "freckles" on lion's muzzle.

3. To assemble mouse, glue yarn tail at lower right side of body back. Glue or sew edges of body pieces together, leaving bottom edge open. Fold mouse ears at fold line and glue. Position and glue ear to head back. Glue head front to body front overlapping felt 1/2". Glue head back to body back. Glue second ear and wiggle eye to head front and a wiggle eye on head back so that mouse can be seen from either side. Cut two pieces of thread 3" long and glue center of pieces to tip of mouse's nose. Glue pompom over thread. Glue second pompom nose on reverse side.

See photo on page 6

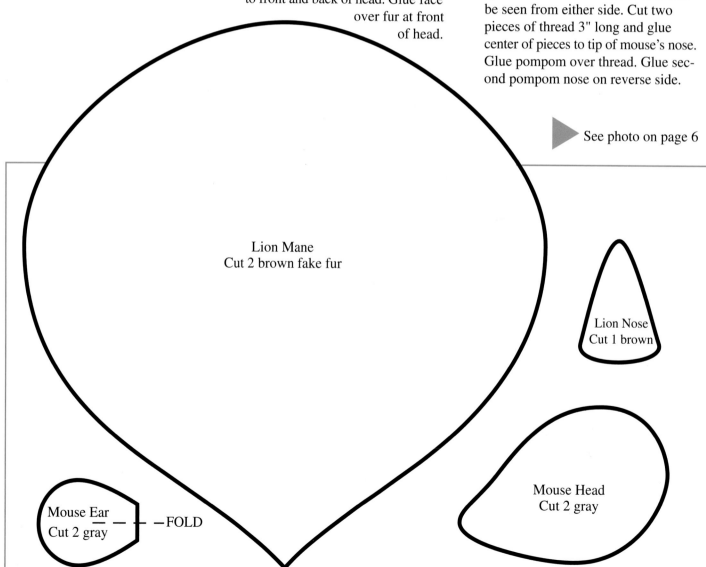

Lion Mane
Cut 2 brown fake fur

Lion Nose
Cut 1 brown

Mouse Head
Cut 2 gray

Mouse Ear
Cut 2 gray — — — —FOLD

Three Little Kittens

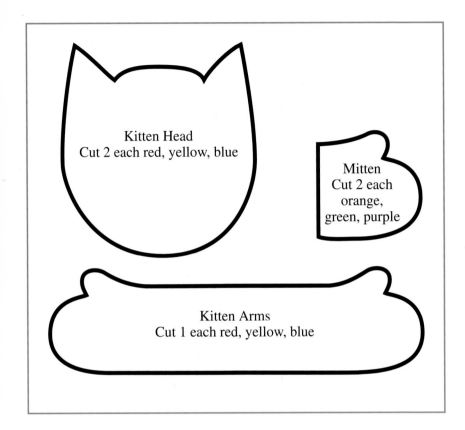

Materials:

- felt
  - 9"x12" sheets—dark blue, red and yellow
  - 4"x4"—green, orange and purple
- dimensional paint, black and yellow
- tacky or hot glue
- thread (optional) red, yellow and dark blue

Instructions:

1. **Felt Cutting Guide:** Cut two size C body shapes, two head shapes and one arm piece from dark blue, red and yellow felt. Cut two mittens from green, orange and purple felt.

2. Position (see photo on page 3) and glue blue arm piece on blue body shape. Glue or sew edges of blue body shapes together with arm piece between them, leaving bottom edge open. Glue blue head shape to body front, overlapping 1/2". Glue head back to body back.

3. Repeat Step 2 to make red and yellow kittens. Glue mittens to kittens' arms.

4. Paint eyes, nose and whiskers on one side of blue kitten's head with yellow dimensional paint. Let dry. Repeat on other side. Use black dimensional paint to draw faces on front and back of red and yellow kittens.

 See photo on page 3

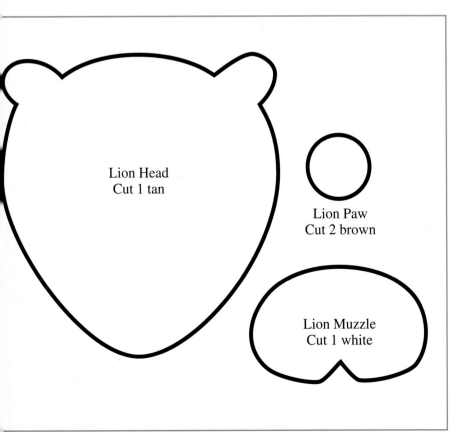

The Owl and the Pussycat

Materials:

- felt
  9"x12" sheets—gray, green, white
  6"x9"—lavender, pink and red
- dimensional paint, black and white
- gold jump ring, 8mm
- 3" of white lace, 1 1/4" wide
- pink pompom, 1/2"
- 7" of red ribbon, 1/4" wide
- pair of wiggle eyes, 10mm
- pair of wiggle eyes, 7mm
- tacky or hot glue
- thread (optional), pink, gray and purple

Instructions:

1. Felt Cutting Guide:
From **gray** felt cut two owl shapes and three tree trunks. From **white** felt cut island, moon, stars, owl face shape, guitar circle and one fruit. From **green** felt cut boat, tree foliage and guitar. From **pink** felt cut two pig body shapes, two pig head shapes and one fruit. From **red** felt cut two owl wings, owl beak, and two fruits. From **lavender** felt cut two size C body shapes (see page 19) and two cat head shapes (see page 27) and one fruit.

2. To make owl, glue or sew edges of owl body shapes together leaving the bottom edge open. Glue owl face pieces (white and red) to owl face. Glue guitar circle to guitar and guitar to body front. Glue wings to body front and larger wiggle eyes to face.

3. To make pig, glue or sew edges of pig body shapes together leaving the bottom edge open. Glue pig head front to body overlapping 1/2". Glue head back to body back. Glue eyes

and pompom to face. Glue jump ring to pompom. Use black dimensional paint to draw mouth and nostrils on pompom and let dry.

4. To make pussycat, wrap lace around cat body front with ends tucked behind it. Glue or sew edges of body front to back, leaving bottom edge open. Glue head to body front

overlapping felt 1/2". Glue cat head to body back. Use white dimensional paint to draw pussycat face—eyelids, nose and whiskers—and let dry. Tie a small bow with red ribbon, trim ends and glue bow next to pussycat's ear.

5. For bong tree, glue fruit to foliage. Glue three trunks to back of foliage.

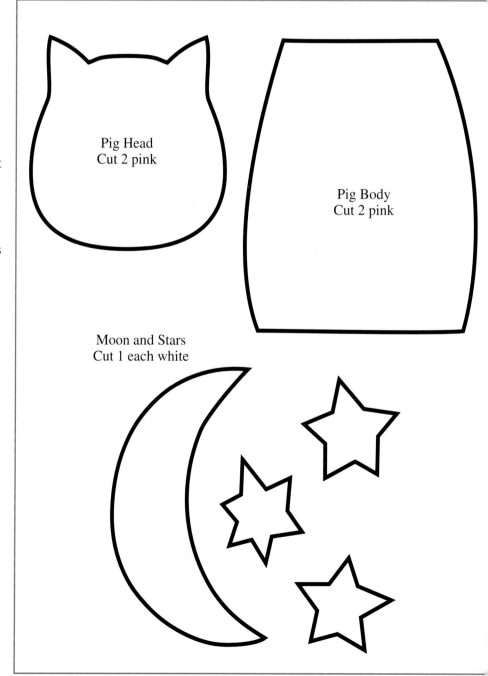

Pig Head
Cut 2 pink

Pig Body
Cut 2 pink

Moon and Stars
Cut 1 each white

 See photo on page 5

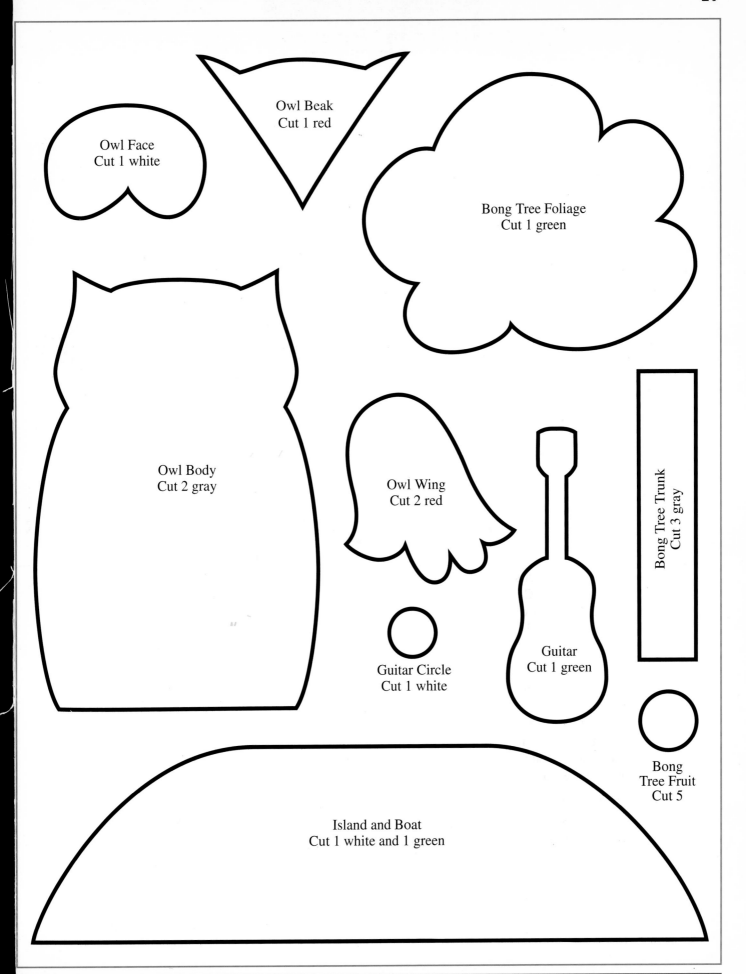

Owl Face
Cut 1 white

Owl Beak
Cut 1 red

Bong Tree Foliage
Cut 1 green

Owl Body
Cut 2 gray

Owl Wing
Cut 2 red

Bong Tree Trunk
Cut 3 gray

Guitar Circle
Cut 1 white

Guitar
Cut 1 green

Bong
Tree Fruit
Cut 5

Island and Boat
Cut 1 white and 1 green

Pattern and Instructions for

Ben Bear

Materials:

■ felt
  two 9"x12" sheets—tan
  9"x12" sheet—yellow
  6"x6"—light beige and red

■ 8"x11" of fusible interfacing

■ pompoms
  one 1", tan
  one 7mm, red
  three 7mm, black
  three 7mm, green

■ 6" beige Velcro, 3/4" wide

■ tacky or hot glue

■ thread (optional), tan

Instructions:

1. **Felt Cutting Guide:**
From **tan** felt, cut one bear body front, one body back (see page 20 for body pattern) and two ears. From **yellow** felt, cut two pockets. From **light beige**, cut two bear paws and one bear tummy. Following manufacturer's instructions, iron fusible interfacing onto back of **yellow** felt and cut coat and hat. Iron on back of **red** felt and cut two boots.

2. Glue ears to body back. Sew or glue edges of body front and back together, leaving bottom edge open. Glue tan pompom to face for muzzle. Glue two black pompoms to face for eyes and one on muzzle for nose. Glue red pompom to bottom of muzzle for tongue. Glue bear's tummy and paws in place.

3. Glue pockets on raincoat. Glue green pompoms on coat for buttons. Glue 2" Velcro strip on bear's chest and matching piece on back of raincoat. Glue 1" strips of Velcro on bear's feet and head; glue matching Velcro pieces on backs of boots and hat.

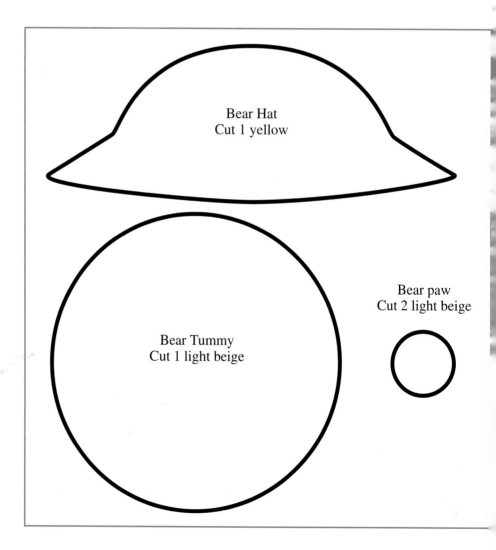

Bear Hat
Cut 1 yellow

Bear paw
Cut 2 light beige

Bear Tummy
Cut 1 light beige

See photo on page 10

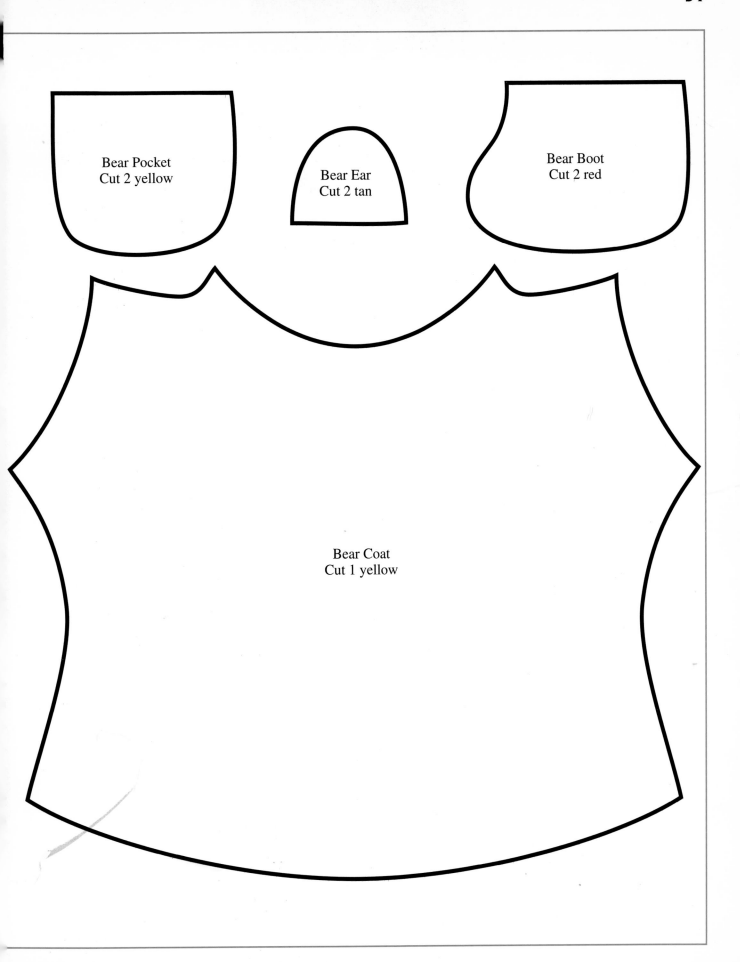

Bear Pocket
Cut 2 yellow

Bear Ear
Cut 2 tan

Bear Boot
Cut 2 red

Bear Coat
Cut 1 yellow

Moon Creatures

Materials:

- felt
    9"x12" sheet—neon green
    6"x9"—neon orange, neon
      pink, and lavender
    very small scrap of hot pink
- one wiggle eye, 20mm
- one wiggle eye, 12mm
- three wiggle eyes, 10mm
- glue
- thread (optional) green, orange and pink

Instructions:

1. **Felt Cutting Guide:**
From **green** felt cut two size C body shapes (see page 19 for pattern), two MC#1 head shapes, two MC#2 head shapes, four MC#1 arms and two antennae (felt strips 1/4"x1 1/2"). From **neon pink** felt cut two size C body shapes. From **orange** felt cut two size C body shapes, two MC#3 head shapes and two MC#3 arms. From **lavender** felt cut two MC#1 arms, two MC#2 arms and two MC#3 arms. From hot pink felt cut two small circles (5/8"). Option: Cut geometric shapes to create your own original Moon Creatures.

2. For all moon creatures, position and glue arm pieces to body backs. Glue or sew edges of body fronts and backs, leaving bottom edges open. Glue head front to body front, overlapping felt 1/2".

3. For moon creature #1, glue antennae between head front and back. Glue head back to body back. For moon creature #2 glue circle hands to ends of arms. Glue eyes on heads.

▶ See photo on page 8

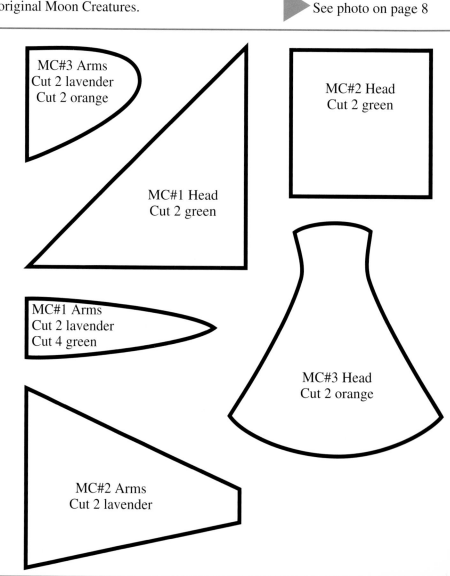

MC#3 Arms
Cut 2 lavender
Cut 2 orange

MC#2 Head
Cut 2 green

MC#1 Head
Cut 2 green

MC#1 Arms
Cut 2 lavender
Cut 4 green

MC#3 Head
Cut 2 orange

MC#2 Arms
Cut 2 lavender

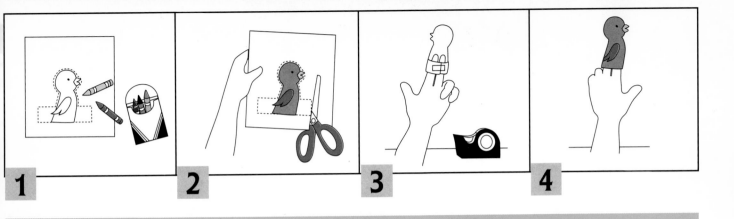

1 **2** **3** **4**

Fussy Baby with the Brand New Tooth

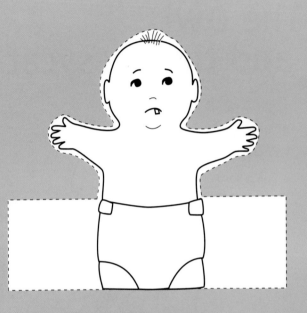

"This is Spot who licks the baby's toes

     Slurp! Slurp! Slurp!

to cheer up Fussy Baby with the brand new tooth.

Ha! Ha! Ha!   That tickles."

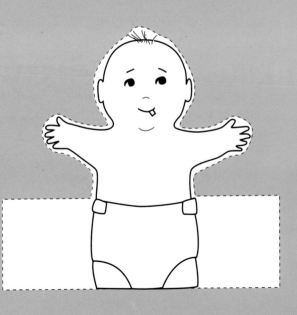

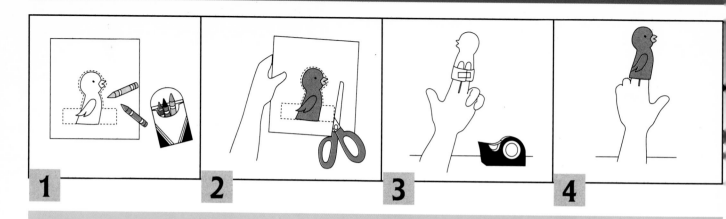

1 **2** **3** **4**

The Owl
and the Pussycat

"The owl and the Pussycat went to sea
In a beautiful pea-green boat..."

I Like Little Pussy

"I like little pussy, her coat is so warm;

And if I don't hurt her, she'll do me no harm.

So I'll not pull her tail, nor drive her away,

But pussy and I very gently will play.

She shall sit by my side and I'll give her some food;

And she'll love me because I am gentle and good."

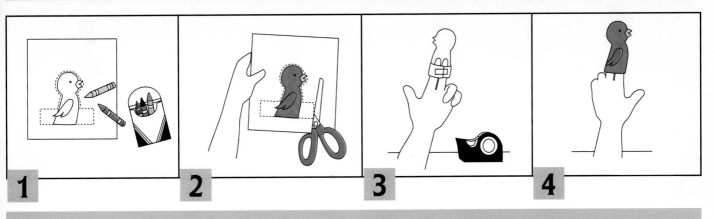

1 **2** **3** **4**

Moon Creatures Party

"Way, way up in the night time sky,
    Moon creatures dance and eat moon pie."

Five Little Monkeys

"No more monkeys jumping on the bed!"

Three Billy Goats Gruff

"Big Billy Goat Gruff trip-tropped up to the hills to join
his brothers where they nibbled the grass that grew
thick and sweet until all three grew big and fat."